If I REALLY WANTED TO

MAKE A
DIFFERENCE

I WOULD . . .

RACINE, WI

If I Really Wanted to Make a Difference, I Would . . .
ISBN: 979-8-88898-115-3 - *Paperback*
ISBN: 979-8-88898-117-7 - *Hardcover*
ISBN: 979-8-88898-116-0 - *Ebook*
Copyright © 2023 by Honor Books
Racine, WI

Cover design, interior design, and editing by Faille Schmitz.

Manuscript prepared by Moira Allaby, Florissant, Colorado.

INTRODUCTION

We're here for only a while, and then we're gone. Do our lives matter? Is it possible to make a difference in the world around us? Can one person really change anything?

The answer to those questions is yes! Every life matters. One person can certainly change things. And the question is not "if" we will make a difference in this world, but rather what kind of difference will that be? Will we impact the world around us for good or for evil?

The simple suggestions contained in this small book are designed to provide opportunities for you to make a solid contribution for good. Whether that contribution sweeps the planet or changes one moment of one life for the better, you will have created a lasting legacy and your life will have made a difference.

God bless you in your quest!

IF I REALLY WANTED TO
MAKE A DIFFERENCE,
I WOULD . . .

TALK LESS AND LISTEN MORE

Truly listening to another person is a gift—the ultimate sign of respect for another's thoughts. But it's a difficult gift to give. Instead of listening, we may be wondering what we should do later in the day or what we should say next. The bottom line is that most of us are simply too self-absorbed to be good listeners.

Listening is a skill that requires practice and determination. To master it, you must be willing to close your mouth and consciously focus on the other person's words. Becoming a good listener is hard work, but giving the gift of being heard can make a great difference in the lives of those around you.

My beloved brethren, let every man be swift to hear, slow to speak.

JAMES 1:19 KJV

IF I REALLY WANTED TO
MAKE A DIFFERENCE,
I WOULD ...

GET
ENOUGH
REST

SLEEPING IS NOT A CRIME; IN FACT IT CAN BE SUBLIME.

Our culture seems to value activity much more than rest—quick response and action much more than contemplation and repose. It's no wonder many of us feel muddled, overwhelmed, and just plain tired. Burning the candle at both ends may seem virtuous, but too often it has negative results, especially in our relationships with others.

Begin to view rest as a gift from God, a way to process your thoughts and rejuvenate your soul. Those who think this way experience an increasing sense of well-being, which overflows to those around them. It's a much more effective way to make a difference.

The morning is wiser than the evening.

RUSSIAN PROVERB

IF I REALLY WANTED TO
MAKE A DIFFERENCE,
I WOULD . . .

PUT
PEOPLE
FIRST

Relationships are work. Whether we're dealing with family members, friends and acquaintances, or business associates, developing and sustaining relationships takes time and effort. Yet those same relationships can be the greatest source of joy and inspiration in our lives. It just makes sense to put people at the top of our priority lists.

Determine to write a note, place a phone call, or arrange for a visit with someone in your life. Imagine what a difference you can make in the world by investing in the lives of those around you. That won't happen unless you make it happen. Begin today to put people first in your life.

There is no joy, except in human relations.

SAINT-EXUPERY

REFUSE TO HOLD GRUDGES

It's easy to hold on to hurt, to store it away. Sometimes we don't even realize we are nursing a grudge because the feelings are so deeply lodged in our hearts. Yet a grudge affects us and everyone around us. It can lead to bitterness, stunt our emotional growth, and weaken our relationships.

Letting go of resentment will make you a better person, but that's only half the miracle. When you take the next step and express absolute forgiveness, you emulate God and make way for restoration and freedom in the life of another person. What a remarkable opportunity to change your world!

Bear with each other and forgive whatever grievances you may have against one another.

COLOSSIANS 3:13

IF I REALLY WANTED TO
MAKE A DIFFERENCE,
I WOULD . . .

BE ON TIME

SOMEONE ELSE'S TIME IS A TERRIBLE THING TO WASTE.

We all know the frustration of waiting for someone who is late for an appointment. We feel irritated and stressed, especially if we have rearranged our own schedule and rushed through traffic to be at the appointed meeting place on time. Of course we are all late on occasion due to circumstances beyond our control. But chronic lateness demonstrates a lack of respect for others by robbing them of life's most precious commodity—time.

Determine to make a difference in the lives of others by showing that you value them and treasure the time they have agreed to spend with you. Schedule realistically and give yourself enough time to accommodate traffic and unexpected delays. Small considerations mean a lot.

There is one kind of robber whom the law does not strike at . . . who steals what is most precious to men: time.

NAPOLEON I

CHOOSE FRIENDS OF VARIOUS AGES IN VARYING SITUATIONS

FRIENDS ARE THE SPICE OF LIFE.

I n the *New York Times* bestseller, *Tuesday's with Morrie*, a young man, Mitch, returns to visit an old professor, Morrie, who is dying. Through weekly visits, their friendship grows and deepens, and Mitch learns how to truly live.

It's a natural tendency to put people into categories: the middle aged, the elderly, the disabled, the dying. Categorizing people can seem tidy. And yet, there is really nothing "tidy" about life. This unfortunate technique will limit your friendships and could keep you from meeting someone who would challenge, inspire, and comfort you—even bring much joy and laughter to your life. God created you with the capacity to make a difference by giving of yourself. If you want to *truly live*, open yourself to friendships with people outside your present age and station in life.

Acquaintance I would have, but when't depends
Not on the number, but the choice of friends.

ABRAHAM COWLEY

IF I REALLY WANTED TO
MAKE A DIFFERENCE,
I WOULD . . .

AVOID NEGATIVE THINKING

Negativity and cynicism seem to be in fashion. Most of us don't realize how much it affects our lives and the lives of those around us. Even our body language can convey powerful messages. Negative thoughts become attitudes and words that do nothing but steal joy from our lives—and possibly from the lives of others as well.

It's difficult, though, when faced with so much of the seeming unfairness in life, to respond positively. And you certainly wouldn't want to appear carelessly trite by denying true misfortune or pain. Positive thinking is all in the approach. If you choose to abandon negativity and approach life with optimism, quite likely people in your life will respond in kind.

An anxious heart weighs a man down, but a kind word cheers him up.

PROVERBS 12:25

IF I REALLY WANTED TO
MAKE A DIFFERENCE,
I WOULD . . .

TAKE MORE PICTURES

PICTURES ARE LITTLE FRAMES OF TIME.

Time flies—especially as we get older. The enormous amount of stimuli we encounter each day makes it increasingly difficult to absorb the moment. Taking pictures of special occasions —birthdays, anniversaries, reunions with family and old friends—helps mark those times in our minds. Sending copies to people will allow them to cherish those occasions as well.

You can make a wonderful difference for generations to come by preserving cherished memories on film. You can also help your children appreciate the progression of life by showing them photographs of themselves, their friends, and their family members at different ages. Becoming an amateur photographer is neither difficult nor expensive. It's a gift that will keep your family laughing and bonding year after year after year.

To be able to enjoy one's past life is to live twice.

MARTIAL

IF I REALLY WANTED TO
MAKE A DIFFERENCE,
I WOULD . . .

TAKE AN ELDERLY PERSON OUT TO DINNER

GOOD MEAL, GOOD CONVERSATION, GREAT MEMORY.

A meal with a friend may be something we enjoy often and take for granted, but it can be a wonderful gift to an elderly person who has limited income or can no longer drive. It's also a gift that often pays unexpected dividends to the giver in terms of friendship and the wisdom that comes only through life experience.

If you have a friend, neighbor, or family member who seldom has an opportunity to get out, you can make an important difference by offering to take them out to lunch or dinner, to a social event, or even to run errands. What begins as a simple act of kindness will almost certainly become an enriching experience in both of your lives.

Age is opportunity no less
Than youth itself, though in another dress.

HENRY WADSWORTH
LONGFELLOW

REMEMBER

SPECIAL

OCCASIONS

CELEBRATIONS ARE THE WELLSPRINGS OF LIFE.

Special occasions are markers in life. They cause us to pause and remember. Holidays are times for family to gather and step out of the everyday. With graduation or retirement, we take time to mark accomplishments and milestones. We give honor and acknowledge the dawning of a new era. Weddings, birthdays, and showers allow us to share in the joy of life's adventures: a marriage, a new year, a new life.

A recently married woman cited some advice that she received regarding her wedding: "Take in your special day with all five senses. Don't let any part of the magic slip past you." Make a difference in your life and the lives of others by refusing to let the busyness of the occasions keep you from truly living them. Will yourself to savor every moment!

These are the Lord's appointed feasts, the sacred assemblies you are to proclaim at their appointed times.

LEVITICUS 23:4

IF I REALLY WANTED TO
MAKE A DIFFERENCE,
I WOULD . . .

OFFER
FREE
BABYSITTING

MANY OF LIFE'S MOST VALUABLE GIFTS ARE TIME AND ENERGY.

Most parents would agree that they have never experienced anything that brought so much satisfaction *and* so much bone-tired weariness as parenting. Just the details of the day can be consuming—lunches, soccer practice, carpooling, homework, and much more. Schedules can become so hectic that parents have little time for nurturing their own relationship or anchoring their own souls.

What a difference you can make in the life of a tired parent by providing a break for the day or a night out to have some fun and reenergize. A gift of personal time is one of the most thoughtful and valuable gifts you can give. Giving it will make you feel as good as the person who receives it.

One who knows how to show and to accept kindness will be a friend better than any possession.

SOPHOCLES

IF I REALLY WANTED TO
MAKE A DIFFERENCE,
I WOULD . . .

CELEBRATE

DIVERSITY

Different is Good!

I n a recent discussion, a man reared in New England said, tongue in cheek, "Different is bad." No matter where we're from, it's a normal tendency to act or think in ways that reinforce this nonsensical concept. Young children are often taught to conform to a "type." We grow up thinking the status quo is the best. When we look at ourselves and the world around us, however, we can't deny that God has created a universe that celebrates diversity.

If you wish to follow the pattern God has set in place, you will do more than tolerate difference, you will learn to embrace it. You can literally change your world by challenging and encouraging those around you to develop their unique gifts and abilities, experience the richness of cultural differences, and open their minds to ideas and concepts other than their own.

If the whole body were an eye, where would the sense of hearing be? If the whole body were an ear; where would the sense of smell be?

1 Corinthians 12:17

LIVE IN THE PRESENT

CHANGE IS POSSIBLE ONLY IN THE PRESENT.

I n Arthur Miller's *Death of a Salesman*, Willy Loman is a man who won't face reality. He lives in the past, constantly reminiscing, always looking back. His obsession with life as it used to be has caused him to lose his grasp on the life in the present and has robbed him of his dreams for the future. His opportunity to make a difference with his life was wasted.

Living your life in the past is not only sad, it's dangerous. Why? Because you can have no effect on the past. It is what it is. Dwelling on it will only leave you frustrated and stagnant. But focusing on the present opens up a world full of possibilities.

Lying to ourselves is more deeply ingrained
than lying to others.

DOSTOYEVSKY

IF I REALLY WANTED TO
MAKE A DIFFERENCE,
I WOULD . . .

READ A BOOK TO A CHILD

From the high-hat, high jinks of Dr. Seuss' *Go, Dog. Go!* to the enchanted nighttime land of *Where the Wild Things Are*, hearing a good story propels a child's mind into regions that the adult mind seldom enters. Children are, by nature, creatures of fantasy, weaving tales and creating pretend scenarios that guide their play. When we read to children, not only does it expand their minds, but it fulfills and enhances their imaginations—the fertile soil in which dreams of greatness germinate and sprout.

Make a difference by picking up some of your favorite children's books, finding yourself a child—or two or three—and reading! You'll not only be engaging and teaching a child for a moment, you will be helping that child build thoughts and shape ideas for the future.

A book is good company.

HENRY WARD BEECHER

IF I REALLY WANTED TO
MAKE A DIFFERENCE,
I WOULD . . .

TELL THE
PEOPLE
IN MY LIFE
HOW I FEEL
ABOUT THEM

LOVING WORDS FROM THE HEART ARE NEVER FORGOTTEN.

As children we seem to have no problem expressing our feelings for others. But along the road to adulthood, we often lose that wonderful childlike gift. We become inhibited and awkward, reluctant to tell even those closest to us how much we love and respect them. We hope they are picking up our good vibes or noticing our gratuitous acts. We want them to read between the lines. But somehow, we can't seem to find the simple words that would make our message clear.

This reluctance to put feelings into words is unfortunate because words have power. And combined with expressions of the heart, they leave an indelible impact on the lives of others. You can make a difference in the strength and resilience of your relationships simply by affirming those you care about. Speak up! You'll be glad you did.

Talk not of wasted affection; affection never was wasted.

HENRY WADSWORTH LONGFELLOW

IF I REALLY WANTED TO
MAKE A DIFFERENCE,
I WOULD . . .

KEEP IN TOUCH WITH MY FRIENDS

FRIENDSHIP DOUBLES YOUR FIELD OF INFLUENCE.

According to the Girl Scout song, "Make New Friends," old friends are like "gold." Fine gold is wrought by a refining fire, which makes the Scout reference all the more appropriate. For lasting friendships are certainly developed through a unique refining process.

Old friends have had the opportunity to see you at your best, worst, and every state in between. They know what makes you tick and appreciate how far you have come. They understand your flaws and love you anyway. Appreciate the friends who have made a difference in your life, and ask yourself if knowing you made a difference in theirs. Celebrating those relationships will help you see how one life can affect another.

Forsake not an old friend, for a new one does not compare with him.

ECCLESIASTES 9:10 APOCRYPHA

IF I REALLY WANTED TO
MAKE A DIFFERENCE,
I WOULD . . .

BE CAREFUL
NOT TO
OVERCOMMIT

THINK BEFORE YOU COMMIT!

B usyness. It's a modern-day malady that turns good, kind people into grouches. We become half-humans racing from obligation to obligation. Pouring ourselves out all over the place leaves us with—a mess.

You won't be able to make a positive difference in your world if you are exhausted and scattered and constantly in a frenzy. Learn when to say yes and when to say no. Remember that it's possible to work yourself into an early grave without ever doing anything of real value. Don't waste your life chasing after mindless busyness. Leave a lasting legacy by thoughtfully considering commitments before you make them.

One cannot manage too many affairs; like pumpkins in the water, one pops up while you try to hold down the other.

CHINESE PROVERB

IF I REALLY WANTED TO
MAKE A DIFFERENCE,
I WOULD . . .

HAVE DINNER AT HOME AT THE TABLE, WITH MY FAMILY

Bread is best when served with conversation.

A recent study done by an educational group revealed that children who ate at least two meals, five days a week with their families performed better in school and were better adjusted socially. Mealtime can serve not only as a means of including veggies in the daily intake but as a forum where family can feel free to talk about the day, what lies ahead, and possibly even joke a bit.

In that short time together, you will be providing a heightened sense of family connectedness and investing in the future well-being of your children. You will also be making memories. You will be building a rapport for communication that will serve you well during the difficult times that come to every family. Make a difference in the life of your family—eat together!

Whoever makes home seem to the young dearer and more happy is a public benefactor.

Henry Ward Beecher

IF I REALLY WANTED TO
MAKE A DIFFERENCE,
I WOULD . . .

KEEP A STASH OF GREETING CARDS

CARDS ARE MAIL WITH HEART.

It seems as if there's a greeting card for every occasion—and, as a major card company has announced, an occasion for every person (or pet). It's funny, at a time when we can choose from a variety of quick and convenient ways to communicate that there would be such a demand for a paper product intended to be delivered by snail mail. But people always seem to enjoy receiving a card along with the credit card bills and second-mortgage offers.

An encouraging card can help you make a difference in the life of a person who is going through a difficult time. It's a wonderful way to cheer up a sick friend or brighten the day of a harried mother with small children. Elderly people love to receive cards too. The truth is that we all do. Touch someone's life today. Send a card!

I thank my God every time I remember you.

PHILIPPIANS 1:3

IF I REALLY WANTED TO
MAKE A DIFFERENCE,
I WOULD . . .

RETURN
PHONE
CALLS

Reach out and return that call.

The telephone has become our closest companion and most despised intrusion. In our information-rich world, no one would see it as less than a necessary evil. To make matters worse, answering machines garner messages even when we aren't around. Calls that we once would have simply missed now must be returned—more entries on our already-too-full "to do" list.

Miss Manners would say that returning a call is polite. Picking up the phone and calling back says, "I respect you, and I'm recognizing that you took time out of your life to dial my number." What's more, that call may mean a conversation that will bring sunshine into the life of another person. Begin to think of returning phone messages as an opportunity to make a difference.

The best of life is conversation.

Ralph Waldo Emerson

IF I REALLY WANTED TO
MAKE A DIFFERENCE,
I WOULD . . .

REFUSE TO GET RATTLED ON THE ROAD

STIFLE THE RAGE; DRIVE FRIENDLY.

A recent TV report focused on a particular traffic jam. Two cars on the side of the road. Police involved. What led to this major tie-up? Road Rage. The news anchor reported "road rage" as if it were as natural as having a morning cup of coffee.

Whether or not we're people given to volatility on the road, driving can certainly raise our blood pressure. But why let it? You could be the kind soul who lets the impatient driver in. You could give the motorist who's been riding your bumper for the past five miles an opening to pass. Give a person "the nod" or "the wave" when he's courteous on the road. You can make a difference even in rush-hour traffic.

In the arena of human life, the honors and rewards fall to those who show their good qualities in action.

ARISTOTLE

IF I REALLY WANTED TO
MAKE A DIFFERENCE,
I WOULD . . .

LIVE
IN THE
MOMENT

YOUR LIFE CONSISTS OF MOMENTS; DON'T WASTE THEM.

Many of us are so fixed on future happiness that we miss the peace and contentment available to us in the present. Instead of savoring the moment, we set our focus on our next goal—and the next—and the next. This attitude keeps us plodding through life, always seeking but never finding lasting fulfillment.

Do you wish to motivate and inspire others? Do you long to make a difference in the lives of those around you? If so, you must learn to live in the moment, because that's where the opportunities are. That's where you find the time to share your experiences with others. That's where relationships are built and nurtured. That's where true values are established and passed on. That's where real life takes place.

Do not boast about tomorrow, for you do not know what a day may bring forth.

PROVERBS 27:1

BE CAREFUL NOT TO ASSIGN BLAME

BLAME IS THE VOICE OF COWARDICE.

When God approached Adam and Eve after they had disobeyed Him, they readily admitted their indiscretion—well, not exactly! The truth is that avoiding personal responsibility by placing blame is an age-old strategy that can be traced all the way back to the Garden of Eden. Adam brushed it off on Eve. Eve made the serpent her scapegoat.

It takes humility and courage to own up to our mistakes and admit that we are (go ahead, you can say it), "*wrong*." It isn't an easy thing to do. But taking responsibility for your actions and refusing to pass the blame to someone else can make a big difference in your life and the lives of others. It engenders respect and builds character. Take a lesson from Adam.

One must first learn to live oneself before one blames others.

DOSTOYEVSKY

IF I REALLY WANTED TO
MAKE A DIFFERENCE,
I WOULD . . .

LEARN PEOPLE'S NAMES

What's in a Name? Everything!

E xperts say that repeating someone's name three times will embed it in the mind. This technique also requires us to focus on the individual we are being introduced to. It's easy in social situations to become so preoccupied with our own insecurities that we simply fail to really connect with the person in front of us.

It may seem like a small concern, but small concerns can make a big difference. Taking the time to learn and remember someone's name says that you find that person worthy of the effort, important enough to be noticed and acknowledged. It is, in a real way, an act of kindness and respect. When you meet someone for the first time, take a good look at the face and use the name—three times for good measure. Little things mean a lot.

It is common to forget a man and slight him if his good will cannot help you.

Plautus

WEIGH MY MOTIVES

WHAT REALLY MATTERS ARE MATTERS OF HEART.

Humans are complicated. This is never truer than when it comes to deciphering our motives. Why do we do what we do? Think what we think? Believe what we believe? What underlies our lives? Why do we find it so important to appear "together," wealthy, intelligent?

What are the motives behind your actions? If you don't know, you might want to do some soul-searching and find out. Interacting with those around you in an honest and forthright manner can make a big difference in the strength and quality of your relationships. Examine your motives often; be honest with yourself. You will find that the fragrance of a pure heart is one of life's greatest pleasures.

As water reflects a face, so a man's heart reflects the man.

PROVERBS 27:19

IF I REALLY WANTED TO
MAKE A DIFFERENCE,
I WOULD . . .

DEAL
WITH MY
INSECURITIES

ARE YOUR INSECURITIES IN THE DRIVER'S SEAT?

People who are secure in their own self-image make the best advocates and friends because they aren't always concerned with what others think of them. They can focus on relationships and situations with confidence. They are free to be themselves.

Are you plagued by insecurities? Don't let them cripple your relationships and cause you to react in unbecoming ways. Deal with them head-on. Affirm yourself with the knowledge that God made you a unique and wondrous individual. You will be amazed to see how different your life and relationships will be when you have learned to lose the insecurities and revel in the person you are.

A healthy self-image is seeing yourself as God sees you—no more and no less.

JOSH MCDOWELL

If I really wanted to
Make a Difference,
I would . . .

Be the
First to say,
"I'm Sorry."

"SORRY" IS BEST SAID WITH THE HEART AND WITH THE HEAD.

Not much in life makes us want to dig in our heels more than having to apologize, especially if the other person is even more at fault and hasn't apologized. Most of us bristle at the idea. We want to give a quick, less than heartfelt, "Sorry," and be done with it. It takes courage to be the first to apologize in any situation. But if we apologize, specifically and with sincerity, it can bring great healing.

If you find yourself in this difficult place, you have an opportunity to make a difference, to turn the tide of resentment and alienation. In that sense, you have taken control of the situation. Don't let fear or pride paralyze you. Stand up and become the better person. At least one life will be changed—your own!

To no kind of begging are people so averse, as to begging pardon.

JULIUS CHARLES HARE AND AUGUSTUS WILLIAM HARE

IF I REALLY WANTED TO
MAKE A DIFFERENCE,
I WOULD . . .

REFUSE TO LET PEOPLE WALK ON ME

RESPECT IS A GIFT YOU MUST FIRST GIVE YOURSELF.

The Bible says that God created us in His own image, unique and priceless in all His creation. When we allow others to treat us badly or disrespectfully, we are really allowing them to denigrate our Creator as well.

Many people mistake character traits such as humility and meekness for imperatives to serve as doormats for users and pushy, steamroller types. Those traits, when rightly defined, are actually powerful action words that denote a decision to put the needs of others first. They refer to a lack of selfishness rather than a lack of dignity. You will never be able to make a difference in this world unless you respect yourself and others.

God created man in his own image, in the image of God he created him.

GENESIS 1:27

EXPECT THE BEST FROM OTHERS

Too often we carelessly speak negative words into the lives of others. We reinforce natural fears and insecurities that tend to keep others from reaching their full potential. Imagine what a difference we could make in the lives of those around us if we were to make a conscious effort to expect the best and back it up with words of encouragement and praise.

Expecting the best from others will also make a difference in your life. It will guard your heart and mind from cynicism and resentment, engendering a greater sense of well-being and personal happiness. Your relationships will become deeper and stronger. Sure, some people will disappoint you, but a great many more will respond to your expectations by rising to new levels of character and accomplishment.

He too serves a purpose who only stands and cheers.

HENRY ADAMS

IF I REALLY WANTED TO
MAKE A DIFFERENCE,
I WOULD . . .

DO MY PART TO TAKE CARE OF THE PLANET

TAKING CARE OF THE PLANET MAKES LIFE BETTER FOR EVERYONE.

I n a typical day, a person might drive to work alone, drink latte from a disposable cup, and eat lunch from cardboard with plastic ware. These seemingly harmless activities add to the overwhelming amount of pollution in our environment. It's easy to shrug our shoulders and do nothing simply because the problem seems so out of control.

If you really want to make a difference in the health and well-being of future generations, there are environment-conscious things you can do each day! Simple things like recycling garbage bags, cans, bottles, and newspapers; using baking soda rather than harsh chemicals for cleaning floors and counters. The Environmental Protection Agency publishes booklets listing numerous ways average citizens can help stem the tide of pollution. Little changes in the way you live can have a positive effect on the future of this incredible planet.

Everything is perfect coming from the hands of the Creator; everything degenerates in the hands of man.

ROUSSEAU

IF I REALLY WANTED TO
MAKE A DIFFERENCE,
I WOULD . . .

PRAY,
PRAY,
PRAY

B ecause it requires us to place our faith in something more than we can comprehend with our five senses, many people discount prayer as an effective means to positively impact their lives and the lives of those around them. Even for those who appreciate its many benefits, prayer is by nature a mystery, a step in the dark. By all accounts, however, it is also a step in the right direction.

Recent studies in hospitals have confirmed that prayer does make a difference. In a remarkable number of cases, those who were prayed for recovered more quickly from the same ailments than those who did not receive prayer. When was the last time you had a heartfelt conversation with your Creator?

The prayer of a righteous man is powerful and effective.

JAMES 5:16

PROVIDE A MEAL FOR A NEW MOM

A LITTLE KINDNESS GOES A LONG WAY.

"I'm so sleep deprived, I can't even form a complete, uh . . . thought." These words are painfully familiar to every new mother. Enduring the endless napping-feeding-changing cycle, the sudden isolation, and the overwhelming responsibility of caring for another human being around the clock can leave a new mom feeling desperate and depressed. The good news is that a little help goes a long way.

Grocery shopping is difficult for a new mom and preparing a meal can seem like a formidable task. At a time when a nutritious meal can be a boost for everyone in the house, you can make a big difference by preparing a double portion of what you're cooking at home or picking up a nutritious meal from a restaurant or supermarket. When you arrive at the door, you'll probably get a hero's welcome.

Always set a high value on spontaneous kindness.

SAMUEL JOHNSON

IF I REALLY WANTED TO
MAKE A DIFFERENCE,
I WOULD . . .

VALUE
MY
FAMILY

FAMILY FIRST!

We all know the scene in *The Wizard of Oz* where Dorothy clicks her heals together and says three times, "There's no place like home." Like Dorothy, for many of us it takes leaving Kansas to realize just how precious family can be.

Family to you may mean parents and siblings, spouse and children, extended relations, or even a close circle of friends. But before you expend all your energies trying to make a difference in the world at large, take time to focus on those at home. Find ways to encourage and strengthen each one. Be a shoulder to lean on and a good listener. Stand alongside them through good times and tough times. Give them the priceless gift of love and respect. Touching the lives of those you call family will give you a strong platform for reaching out into the world.

Stay, stay at home, my heart, and rest; home-keeping hearts are happiest.

HENRY WADSWORTH LONGFELLOW

73

If I really wanted to
Make a Difference,
I would . . .

Tell
the
Truth

TRUTH IS THE SISTER OF PEACE.

As children, we all heard that honesty is the best policy, but as we grow into adults, that simple truth seems to get clouded. We become masters of half-truths, innuendo, and justification. It's not easy to live with integrity, but if we want to make a lasting difference for good in the lives of others, we must try.

Begin by searching your own heart and being honest with yourself. This can be a much more difficult task than you would imagine. But self-delusion and denial can make you impervious to the truth as it applies to others. It can cause you to fracture relationships and hurt those around you. Make honesty your policy in every aspect of your life. And ask for God's help. He knows you better than you know yourself.

Whoever lives by the truth comes into the light.

JOHN 3:21

IF I REALLY WANTED TO
MAKE A DIFFERENCE,
I WOULD . . .

KEEP MY PRIORITIES STRAIGHT

IT'S EVER-WISE TO PRIORITIZE.

Keeping a healthy balance in our lives is not an easy task. The world we live in is a busy place, filled with choices, obligations, and opportunities. Unless we set priorities in our lives and vigorously maintain them, we are likely to find ourselves hanging on by our fingertips, too involved with survival to affect positive change in the world around us.

Take time to consciously list your obligations and activities, and don't hesitate to put them down on paper. Be as specific as possible. Then honestly and thoughtfully estimate how much time and effort you are devoting to each. This exercise may cause you to see that you are giving less attention to those items that should be most important. You only have one life to live; make it count.

Action should culminate in wisdom.

BHAGAVAD GITA

IF I REALLY WANTED TO
MAKE A DIFFERENCE,
I WOULD . . .

LEARN NOT TO MAKE EXCUSES

THOSE WHO EXCUSE THEIR MISTAKES ARE DOOMED TO REPEAT THEM.

For some people, making excuses has become a bad habit. They drift through life, never quite getting their act together, leaving messes everywhere they go. They are experts at deflecting blame and consequently, they never correct the "stinkin' thinkin'" that caused them to use poor judgment in the first place. They may be saving face temporarily, but in the end, they become big losers.

If you long to make a difference in your world, abandon the practice of making excuses and deflecting blame to others. Take responsibility for your actions and inactions. Own your failures and make them work for you by learning the lessons they teach. You will soon be a stronger, wiser, healthier person—a capable and respected voice in the world.

He who excuses himself accuses himself.

GABRIEL MEURIER

IF I REALLY WANTED TO
MAKE A DIFFERENCE,
I WOULD . . .

BE SENSITIVE
TO THE
LOSSES AND
DISAPPOINTMENTS
OF OTHERS

SOMETIMES "TAKING CARE" IS JUST ABOUT "BEING THERE."

Disappointment and loss are inevitable. Almost every day we encounter someone who is hurting. How we respond to those who are experiencing painful circumstances can make a significant difference in the healing and recovery process. Dr. Ira Byock, an expert on death and dying, gives one critical word of advice to those responding to the suffering of others. "Just show up," he urges.

Even when you don't know what to say, you can "be there." Just your physical presence says, "I care about you and what you are going through." Resist the urge to suggest a quick fix or predict that things will look brighter tomorrow. Don't try to downplay the pain, deny it, or explain it. Instead be a good listener and a strong shoulder. See them through. Selflessly lifting up another person is God's truest work.

The Lord is gracious and righteous; our God is full of compassion.

PSALM 116:5

IF I REALLY WANTED TO
MAKE A DIFFERENCE,
I WOULD . . .

DISCOVER AND USE MY TRUE GIFTS

DON'T HIDE YOUR GIFTS— SOMEONE MIGHT NEED THEM.

I n his book *Growing Strong in the Seasons of Life*, Charles W. Swindoll tells us, "There is only one YOU. Think about that. Your face and features, your voice, your background, your characteristics and peculiarities, your abilities . . . [God] has designed you to be a unique, distinct, significant person." So true! You are God's own creation from head to toe, with your own special gifts and talents.

Those gifts and talents have been placed in your life to help you make a difference in the world around you. They are yours to keep and yours to use as you see fit. Ask God to help you recognize and develop the unique gifting in your life. It will mean hard work and plenty of baby steps. But before long, those gifts will begin to open doors and provide opportunities you never thought possible.

The same man cannot well be skilled in everything; each has his special excellence.

EURIPIDES

IF I REALLY WANTED TO
MAKE A DIFFERENCE,
I WOULD . . .

VARY
MY
ROUTINE

Rise up—usurp the throne from Queen Routine!

Making a difference requires focus and determination. But it also requires flexibility, an openness to new ideas and ways of thinking. Some experts on unleashing potential suggest varying our routines as a way to jostle us out of our usual mind-set. For most, routine is comforting and necessary to help bring order to life. But when routine becomes queen supreme, it not only puts the kabash on our potential, it can also stifle our everyday existence.

How do we know if routine has become queen? If a friend calls you with free tickets to see your favorite artist and you can't go because, of course, Saturday is cleaning day—well, you may be a victim of routine paralysis. Take a look at your routine. If it's got you locked down, it's time to break free. A complete lifestyle probably won't be necessary—just enough to keep yourself in the game.

Habit will reconcile us to everything but change.

Charles Caleb Colton

If I really wanted to
Make a difference,
I would . . .

Refuse
to let
the Little
Things get
to Me

DON'T SWEAT THE SMALL STUFF.

As actress and comedienne Gilda Radner so aptly put it, "It's always something!" Life is filled to overflowing with aggravations, annoyances, slights, and irritations. If we let the little things get us down, we will go through our lives experiencing chronic "downness."

It's tough to make a positive difference when you are viewing life from such a negative vantage point.

If you find yourself becoming wound like a top over little stuff, stop and take some deep breaths. Before you react, ask yourself, "Will this matter in a day? An hour? Half hour? Fifteen minutes?" If the answer is no, shake it off, toss it away, let it go. You'll quickly find your sanity returning and your vision clearing. Make the most of your life by refusing to let the little things get you down.

If you falter in times of trouble, how small is
your strength!

PROVERBS 24:10

IF I REALLY WANTED TO
MAKE A DIFFERENCE,
I WOULD . . .

TEACH-IN ANY CAPACITY

GIVE AND RECEIVE THE GIFT OF LEARNING.

I n his autobiography *Surprised by Joy*, C.S. Lewis tells of a teacher who was instrumental in his education. Lewis says, "Every verse he read turned to music on his lips, something midway between speech and song." This teacher was the first to affirm Lewis's love for poetry and give him an expanded awareness and appreciation.

There's a little bit of "teacher" in each of us. Even if your assignment is to teach a four-year-old how to tie his shoes or a sixteen-year-old how to make a left-hand turn, you will never have a better opportunity to make a difference. Patience and encouragement can bring courage and confidence to the student and a deep sense of satisfaction to the teacher.

A teacher affects eternity; he can never tell
where his influence stops.

HENRY ADAMS

Be Careful
not to
Patronize
the Young
or the Old

PEOPLE ARE FULL OF SURPRISES.

I ndividuals, young and old, have a unique energy, perspective, wisdom, and enthusiasm. In order to allow them to live with the dignity they deserve at every age, it's important for us to lay aside the labels, stereotypes, and preconceptions we routinely connect with certain phases of life.

You can make a wonderful difference in the lives of those around you by refusing to assume that your older friends have less inclination to dream about the future or set challenging goals. In the same way, refuse to assume your younger friends lack certain skills or are bound to act frivolously. Don't make assumptions. Instead, rejoice in the unique path of each life.

Men are but children of a larger growth.

JOHN DRYDEN

IF I REALLY WANTED TO
MAKE A DIFFERENCE,
I WOULD . . .

REMEMBER TO SAY "THANK YOU."

THANK YOU SAYS, "I NOTICE; I UNDERSTAND; I ACKNOWLEDGE."

How wonderful to express, in specific terms, that you noticed and appreciated someone's effort on your behalf. It's a small courtesy that too often is lost in our fast- paced society and one that can make a big difference in the lives of loved ones and strangers alike. Hearing the words "thank you" can restore the joy of serving and ward off cynicism and resentment. Speaking them can guard the heart against arrogance and engender an ongoing appreciation for others.

Never let an opportunity to say "thank you" pass you by. Careful attention to those simple words will strengthen your relationships, open doors of opportunity, and help you appreciate the richness God has placed in your life. Thankfulness is one of the most important habits you can develop and all it takes is a little attention to what is going on around you and practice, practice, practice.

Give thanks in all circumstances.

1 THESSALONIANS 5:18

IF I REALLY WANTED TO
MAKE A DIFFERENCE,
I WOULD . . .

SEND HAND-WRITTEN LETTERS

A HANDWRITTEN LETTER IS A LOVING GIFT THAT NEVER STOPS GIVING.

Modern communication technologies have made the practice of letter writing almost obsolete. What a shame! Consider the impressive letters of Thomas Jefferson, General Robert E. Lee, Emily Dickinson, and so many other great personages. The principles they espoused and their words of wisdom are still making a difference many years after their deaths.

Taking time to sit down and thoughtfully script your thoughts and feelings may seem on the surface to be a waste of time. But doing so creates a unique gift, capable of communicating again and again. Letters filled with encouragement, enlightenment, and wisdom have an almost limitless shelf life—an advantage no contemporary form of communication can offer.

The pen is the tongue of the hand—a silent utterer of words for the eye.

HENRY WARD BEECHER

IF I REALLY WANTED TO
MAKE A DIFFERENCE,
I WOULD . . .

READ
LABELS

EAT SMART!

A national grocery-store chain stocks a brand of "healthy" granola with some suspiciously unhealthy-sounding ingredients, including plyglycerolesters and artificial flavor. Ply-what? Apparently, the word "healthy" is subject to a variety of interpretations. Our health is more precious than gold, and losing it can greatly limit our ability to live life to its fullest and make a difference in the lives of others.

In *Healthy Habits*, David and Anne Frahm say, "Just as the quality of our life is built upon the foundation of good health, the quality of our health is built upon the kinds of foods we feed our bodies." Do your part to maintain good health. Take responsibility for what you eat. Don't be fooled by media hype or marketing devices. Our legislators have mandated that all prepared foods include a list of ingredients. Take time to notice what you are putting into your body.

Tell me what you eat, and I shall tell you what you are.

ANTHELME BRILLAT-SAVARIN

IF I REALLY WANTED TO
MAKE A DIFFERENCE,
I WOULD . . .

REFUSE
TO LIVE
ABOVE MY
MEANS

DEBT IS A CRUEL TASKMASTER.

Easy access to credit and a penchant for instant gratification have made us a nation of debtors. But indebtedness hangs over us like a dark cloud, robs us of opportunities to pursue our dreams, and limits our ability to help others. According to financial advisor Larry Burkett, money is a primary source of friction in many marriages.

Saying no to frivolous debt may seem limiting at first, but in the long run, you will be rewarded with a sense of liberation and empowerment. Don't trade your freedom for some cool new gadget. Save for things worth having and make a conscious choice to forego those purchases you can't afford. You will quickly see a difference in your stress level, your sense of well-being, and your ability to impact the lives of others.

One man pretends to be rich, yet has nothing.

PROVERBS 13:7

Organize and Label Pictures

PHOTOGRAPHS ARE WINDOWS ON THE PAST.

Photographs affirm us in the present by connecting us with the past. They help us understand who we are and from whom we've come. They remind us of the golden moments of everyday life and enhance our sense of connectedness.

You can make a wonderful difference for generations to come by organizing and labeling the golden moments of your family history. It is a gift to yourself, your children, your grandchildren, and all those who will see their faces reflected in the photograph of a relative and feel a renewed sense of identity. When your task has been accomplished, compound your sense of satisfaction by offering to help a friend do the same.

Photographs are precious pieces of life that can be held in the hand.

ROBERTA S. CULLEY

If I really wanted to
make a difference,
I would . . .

Listen to and Chronicle the Lives of my Older Relatives

To RECORD IS TO REMEMBER AND RETELL.

"Do you remember when Nat Sumner jumped on the back of that moving truck that hot summer day and headed north? He was seventeen. Disappeared for three years. . . ." We love rehearsing the antics of the characters who make up our family history. Almost everyone claims a nutty uncle or an aunt with an unusually strong sense of adventure.

You may think that your older relatives will be around forever. But history tells us they won't. When you no longer can listen to their voices, details may slip from your mind. Make a difference for yourself and future generations by seeking out the people who hold your family's precious memories. Write down those family stories in detail. You, and future generations, will be far richer for it.

To forget one's ancestors is to be a brook without a source, a tree without a root.

Chinese Proverb

IF I REALLY WANTED TO
MAKE A DIFFERENCE,
I WOULD . . .

WRITE MY SPOUSE A LOVE LETTER

SEAL YOUR LOVE WITH PEN AND HEART.

There's something poignant about capturing true sentiment on paper. We can tell a spouse we love him or her, but to pen a note of substance requires unlocking the deepest feelings of the heart. What is it about your spouse that causes your heart to skip a beat? Can you name those characteristics that amaze and endear you? That kind of honesty carries with it a certain amount of vulnerability, but it can also make a remarkable difference in your marriage.

Commit your words of love and adoration with pen and paper. Pour out your heart in a way that can be read and appreciated by your spouse over and over again. In the process of composing and recording your words of love, you may find that your feelings for your spouse have become more intense and your commitment is stronger than ever.

Set me as a seal upon thine heart, as a seal upon thine arm.

SONG OF SOLOMON 8:6 KJV

If I REALLY WANTED TO
MAKE A DIFFERENCE,
I WOULD . . .

VOLUNTEER MY TIME FOR SOMETHING I BELIEVE IN

ACTION INFUSED WITH PASSION CAN CHANGE THE WORLD.

Selfless giving fused with enthusiasm is a powerful combination. That's why so many people have chosen volunteerism as a way to make a difference. They have learned that joining with others in order to address a certain need or issue—whether practical or philosophical, local or global—multiplies the degree to which they can affect change. It's also an excellent way to make friends with those who share our interests.

If you have never considered volunteering, the best time to get involved is now. You can teach someone to read, join with others to build a home for a low-income family, cook meals for the elderly and homebound, be a friend and role model to a child, provide transportation to and from doctor visits, clean up a rural highway or neighborhood park—the opportunities are endless. What are you waiting for?

Every calling is great when greatly pursued.

OLIVER WENDELL HOLMES JR.

LET PEOPLE SEE MY TRUE SELF

TRUE SELF-WORTH COMES FROM GOD.

The Bible says that each of us is a complex and unique creation, fashioned by God Himself. It goes on to say that we are unspeakably valuable because our divine Creator made us in His very image. Why is it then that we human beings are so quick to hide our true selves deep inside, fearing that we will be rejected if others see who we really are?

Have you built walls of protection around your life? If so, you will find that those walls do much more than protect you from rejection. They also keep you from reaching out to others and making a difference in their lives. Tear down the walls and come out of hiding. Let your true colors come shining through. You will soon find your understanding and influence expanding.

Everything about you is found in only one individual since man first began—YOU.

CHARLES SWINDOLL

IF I REALLY WANTED TO
MAKE A DIFFERENCE,
I WOULD . . .

GIVE EACH
PERSON
MY FULL
ATTENTION

FOR BEST RECEPTION, TUNE IN.

I s there anything more infuriating than making a point or spilling your guts to someone who isn't really listening? It leaves you feeling foolish and embarrassed. You can make a big difference by giving others your full attention when they need a listening ear.

The next time someone sits down to talk to you, make eye contact often, and listen carefully. Doing so constitutes a truly unselfish act. It isn't necessary to offer advice, just open your heart and mind to hear what is being said. Without saying a word yourself, you will be giving a gift of insight and perspective to someone who is lonely, struggling with a perplexing problem, processing a change, or thinking through a new idea.

One of the best ways to demonstrate God's love is to listen to people.

BRUCE LARSEN

TEACH SOMEONE TO READ

READING IS LIGHT TO GUIDE, ENLIGHTEN, AND ILLUMINATE HOPE.

Reading can be a source of great pleasure, and there is infinite value in the learning it provides. Even casual reading helps to develop the mind. There are many people, however, who cannot read at all. What is life like for someone who is unable to read a road sign or a newspaper article? A simple job application would be daunting, instructions on medication bottles an exercise in futility. Imagine what a difference could be made in the life of such a person simply by teaching him or her the elementary lessons of literacy.

There are centers for literacy where you can help others gain baseline reading skills. Or perhaps you could give your time to coaching a child intent on reading a storybook for the first time. In whatever way you choose to get involved, you will have the satisfaction of knowing you are helping others learn a skill that will serve them every day for the rest of their lives.

Books give not wisdom where was none before,
but where some is, there reading makes it more.

SIR JOHN HARRINGTON

FIND BEAUTY IN EVERY STAGE OF A CHILD'S LIFE

LOOK FOR THE BEAUTY, AND YOU WILL SEE IT.

The "terrible twos" and the "terrible teens" are difficult developmental stages for almost every person. Many parents get so caught up in the confusion and chaos of childhood and adolescent behaviors that they fail to notice or appreciate the day-to-day victories and the beautiful unique qualities just below the surface. It's hard for a parent to be encouraging when they are feeling angry and frustrated.

You can give a loving gift to a young person in your life by making a habit of looking past the acting out and obnoxious self-centered behavior to the beauty waiting to blossom. Youth is fleeting. And yet, it is a critical time for establishing a balanced self- image and positive attitudes. Investing kindness and praise into the life of a child or teenager could be one of the most rewarding things you ever do.

Youth, even in its sorrows, has a brilliancy of its own.

VICTOR HUGO

IF I REALLY WANTED TO
MAKE A DIFFERENCE,
I WOULD . . .

WISH THE
BEST FOR
OTHERS

I f we were *really* honest with ourselves, we'd have to admit that it's sometimes satisfying to see certain people "get theirs." Miss Perfect ends up with a new haircut that would scare Frankenstein, or the office golden boy gets passed over for a promotion. It's natural to have these thoughts. But you can make a difference in your own life and the lives of those around you by choosing to think and do the better thing.

Wishing the best for others and rejoicing in their accomplishments is sometimes difficult, but these attitudes are a safeguard against bitterness, resentment, and cynicism. They keep you focused outward rather than inward. Even better, these attitudes often cause people to respond by becoming better people themselves. Practice wishing the best for others and genuinely celebrating their victories. It's a simple choice. You are sure to find inner peace and deeper character in yourself and others.

Be devoted to one another in brotherly love.
Honor one another above yourselves.

ROMANS 12:10

IF I REALLY WANTED TO
MAKE A DIFFERENCE,
I WOULD . . .

ACT
LIKE AN
ADULT

ADULTS DON'T PLAY CHILDISH GAMES.

How many times a day do we become embroiled in childish situations that drain our energy, stifle our creativity, inhibit our productivity, and cripple our relationships? We can't change other people or insist that they act in a mature manner. But we can control our own responses to immature behavior.

You can begin by refusing to listen to gossip or take sides in personal quarrels. When you find yourself the target of such tactics, you can choose to walk away without responding in kind. Sure, it's tough to ignore childish taunts and provocations. But you can make a difference in your own attitude and the attitudes of others simply by refusing to play the game. Every morning encourage yourself with the following words: *I am an adult, and I intend to act like one.*

Nature, in denying us perennial youth, has at least invited us to become unselfish and noble.

GEORGE SANTAYANA

IF I REALLY WANTED TO
MAKE A DIFFERENCE,
I WOULD . . .

REMEMBER
HOW TO
THINK LIKE
A CHILD

LOOSEN UP, LIGHTEN UP, AND LOVE WITH A CHILD'S HEART.

In the movie *Young Frankenstein*, Gene Wilder is saying good-bye to his sweetheart, Madeline Khan. He steps to embrace her but is immediately rebuffed with, "The hair. The hair." All his attempts to bid her an affectionate adieu are foiled because she doesn't want anything "mussed." That's exactly how some people live their lives. As adults, many of us need the childlike enthusiasm that will allow us to loosen up and live.

You can't make a positive difference in the lives of others by becoming a dreary old fuddy-dud. Engage in some of the activities and thought processes that made childhood so unique. Lie on the ground and watch the clouds roll by, do a cannonball off the diving board, play a game of hide-and-seek with a three-year-old, throw your arms around your loved ones and hug them without reserve. These activities are sure to give you a new lease on life and brighten the world for everyone.

> How beautiful is youth!
> how bright it gleams
> With its illusions,
> aspirations, dreams!
>
> HENRY WADSWORTH LONGFELLOW

PRACTICE
HUMILITY

HUMILITY IS THE BASIS OF GOOD CHARACTER.

In Amy Tan's book *The Joy Luck Club*, four Chinese women with Chinese-American daughters are competing; each wants her daughter to be the most successful. One daughter who appears to be less successful and not as strong as the others confronts what she sees as her mother's disapproval. But her mother tells her that she is the best daughter because she always takes the smallest or least appealing portion. Her constant humility is the best mark of success.

In a society that admires aggressiveness and power, you can make a difference by aspiring to humility. Keeping your feet on the ground and your ego under control will allow you to better enjoy your success, enhance your long-term relationships, and give you a sense of peace and well-being. Buck the tide of pride by living in humility.

Be completely humble and gentle; be patient, bearing with one another in love.

EPHESIANS 4:2

IF I REALLY WANTED TO
MAKE A DIFFERENCE,
I WOULD . . .

ENCOURAGE OTHERS TO PURSUE THEIR DREAMS

INSPIRE SOMEONE TO REACH FOR THE STARS.

D reams can carry people to new heights of achievement. But very often our dreams are trampled by the constant demands of everyday living. We become overwhelmed by self-doubt and lose courage. With time, we lose courage and surrender our dreams to the demons of futility and disappointment.

You can make a wonderful difference by helping others keep their dreams alive. Encourage them to evaluate what practical planning and preparation must take place before their dreams can become reality. Offer consistent input and affirmation. It could be that one day someone you know will find the courage to do something remarkable because you were there to urge them forward.

If you aspire to the highest place, it is no disgrace to stop at the second, or even the third place.

CICERO

IF I REALLY WANTED TO MAKE A DIFFERENCE, I WOULD ...

REFRAIN FROM GIVING UNSOLICITED ADVICE

ADVICE ASKED FOR IS GREATLY VALUED.

An adult daughter constantly tells her mother she "should" do this and "shouldn't" do that. Her exasperated mother finally says, "Honey, for crying out loud, stop 'shoulding' me." This method of imparting our thoughts about how another should live is ineffectual and can damage a relationship. When people talk to us about troubles or even innocuous situations, most often they simply want a sympathetic ear.

Chances are, if you are a great procurer of unsolicited advice, you won't be sought after for the solicited kind. That means you are effectively losing opportunities to make a real difference in the lives of those you care about. Don't throw away your credibility by imposing your advice on others. Hold your tongue, and before long you will find that others are seeking you out.

Teeth placed before the tongue give good advice.

ITALIAN PROVERB

STICK BY A FRIEND IN A CRISIS

A FAIR-WEATHER FRIEND IS NO FRIEND AT ALL.

C ertain friends make us feel great. Being with them is like taking a walk on the first warm day of spring. But how do you feel about taking a walk with them on a cold, stormy, winter day? It's no spring picnic being around a friend who is living through a dark and cold winter, especially if it persists for some time. But loyalty is the essence of deep and lasting friendships.

Let your friends know that you are "there" for them all the time—bright, sunny days and dark, stormy nights. Your loving support may be the healing balm a friend needs to slip out of the darkness and back into the sunshine. Imagine what a difference you can make just by sticking in there during the tough times. You will almost certainly find that same friend at your side during your soul's darkest night.

There is a friend who sticks closer than a brother.

PROVERBS 18:24

IF I REALLY WANTED TO
MAKE A DIFFERENCE,
I WOULD . . .

STAY OUT OF OTHER PEOPLE'S AFFAIRS

Respecting appropriate boundaries is a sign of true friendship.

When it comes to the people we care about, it's always tough to respect their boundaries and let them live their own lives. That's especially true when we see them doing something we feel will cause them unnecessary pain and disappointment. Nevertheless, meddling in the affairs of others only leads to resentment and alienation.

If you want to make a difference in the life of a friend who is in the midst of a difficult situation, offer a shoulder to cry on and a listening ear. But resist the urge to give unsolicited advice or take matters into your own hands. Such actions will compromise your friendship, and you may find yourself labeled the bad guy when all is said and done.

Don't scald your tongue in other people's broth.

English Proverb

IF I REALLY WANTED TO
MAKE A DIFFERENCE,
I WOULD . . .

MENTOR THE PEOPLE WHO WORK FOR ME

Mentoring: Better Boss, Better Employee, Better Company.

Self-confident, capable professionals are those who care about the future potential of those who work for them. These people take time to teach, offer appropriate praise, and provide added responsibility as they see it can be handled. They aren't worried about their employees outshining them. They have learned that mentoring others motivates them to work harder and keeps them loyal to the organization and the professional who has provided instruction and opportunities for growth and advancement.

If you are interested in making a difference in the productivity of your employees and increasing their sense of job satisfaction, draw out and encourage the strengths you see in them. Handing out earned praise and appropriate opportunities for advancement will increase your own success by ensuring that you will get the best from and keep talented, hard-working employees.

It is one of the beautiful compensations of this life that no one can sincerely try to help another without helping himself.

CHARLES DUDLEY WARNER

IF I REALLY WANTED TO
MAKE A DIFFERENCE,
I WOULD . . .

BE THERE
FOR
A SINGLE
PARENT

A SINGLE PARENT CARRIES A DOUBLE RESPONSIBILITY.

Parenting is hard work. Ideally it takes two well-adjusted, loving parents to successfully raise a child. But life isn't ideal. The number of single-parent households continues to increase.

Lending a hand to a friend, neighbor, or family member who is working hard to do a job intended for two is a significant way to make a difference. Many single parents cite finances as their greatest struggle. Perhaps you're in a position to give a check or provide something a child or parent needs. Offering to serve as a backup for child care and transportation are also a big help. But even if you can't provide those things, giving a single parent your moral support can be a precious gift to someone sailing alone on the choppy waters of parenthood.

Carry each other's burdens.

GALATIANS 6:2

IF I REALLY WANTED TO
MAKE A DIFFERENCE,
I WOULD . . .

MAKE MORE JOKES

A MINUTE OF LAUGHTER CAN DISPEL HOURS OF SORROW.

Life is serious business. If you don't think so, open a newspaper or watch the evening news. How can we enjoy life in the midst of natural disasters, human tragedies, and the actions of those whose cold hearts allow them to harm others? There is increasing evidence that laughter can make a big difference. Laughter releases endorphins, increasing a sense of well-being. Many mental-health professionals have found that "laughter therapy" is an effective way to help victims of neglect and abuse.

You may not be the kind of person who feels comfortable cracking jokes, but appreciating the benefits of humor doesn't require you to become a stand-up comic. Begin by looking for the ironies and absurdities in your daily life. Doing so will help you regain perspective and keep your footing on this shaky planet we call home.

The most wasted day is one in which we have not laughed.

SEBASTIEN ROCH NICOLAS CHAMFORT

IF I REALLY WANTED TO
MAKE A DIFFERENCE,
I WOULD . . .

REFUSE TO BELIEVE EVERYTHING I READ AND HEAR

APPROACH INFORMATION WITH HEALTHY SCRUTINY.

Some people say we should believe only fifty percent of what we hear. Sound cynical? Maybe. But taking time to validate information can actually make us more knowledgeable, allaying misconceptions and keeping us tuned in to reality.

A few simple exercises can help you stay on track. First, establish what sources you can trust for accurate information. Second, avoid the lure of sensationalism. Third, make an effort to hear all sides of an issue. Fourth, learn to spot hidden agendas, which can include everything from personal vendettas to corporate profits. What you know can make a difference, so be sure what you know is anchored in the truth.

A man who is always ready to believe what is told him will never do well.

PETRONIUS

IF I REALLY WANTED TO
MAKE A DIFFERENCE,
I WOULD . . .

GIVE

ANONYMOUSLY

NO BAGGAGE ACCOMPANIES AN ANONYMOUS GIFT.

We all like being recognized for the nice things we do. Therefore, many people never experience the deep satisfaction that comes with giving anonymously. As good as it feels to hear "thank you," it feels even better to know that your gift was given freely, with no strings attached. And we shouldn't think of giving only in terms of money. You can enrich the lives of others in many ways—a freshly baked pie left on the doorstep, leaving a note of encouragement in the mailbox, the variations are endless.

If you have never given an anonymous gift, begin by looking for opportunities. Then act! You will quickly find that you are making a difference in the lives of others and even in your own life. And the Bible says that God will reward you for your generosity as well.

"When you give to the needy, do not let your left hand know what your right hand is doing."

MATTHEW 6:3

VISIT A NURSING HOME

TAKE THIS JOURNEY, AND LEARN TO LIVE.

In her book *Another Country*, Mary Pipher explores issues of aging such as physical deterioration and, often as a result, loss of independence. This is never truer than when an elderly person must relinquish his or her home, with its familiarity, possessions, and routines, and move to a nursing home. One ninety-year-old woman said, "You know, in my head and heart, I still feel like a forty-year-old woman. It's my knees that tell me I'm ninety!"

If you know someone who lives in a nursing home, go visit. Take magazines or newspapers—or a favorite food. Just sit for a while and keep them company. If you don't have a friend or relative to visit, check with the closest facility and see how you can volunteer. And ask about bringing your children. It's almost always all right with administrators and a real treat for the residents. Investigate and go. You'll be making a difference in your life and the life of someone else as well.

Life is a country that the old have seen and lived in. Those who have to travel through it can only learn the way from them.

JOSEPH JOUBERT

GIVE MYSELF A BREAK

REACHING TOO FAR CAN CAUSE YOU TO LOSE YOUR GRIP.

L ife is tough for chronic overachievers. They chase after a "to do" list that would be impossible for any normal human being, consistently set themselves up for failure, and live under a dark cloud of guilt and fatigue. Even worse, they often project unrealistic expectations on those around them.

If you are an overachiever, for heaven's sake give yourself a break! It's possible to make a difference in the world without risking your physical and emotional health. Take a serious look at your obligations for the next month and weed out those that can be handled by someone else. Deal with your failures and put them behind you. Set aside time every day for rest and quiet contemplation. And most of all, stop trying to be the Master of the universe. That position has already been filled.

How shall we expect charity towards others, when we are uncharitable to ourselves?

SIR THOMAS BROWNE

DEVELOP MY MIND

A MIND IS A TERRIBLE THING TO WASTE.

I t is widely accepted that potential intelligence is related to heredity, but environment is critical in determining the extent of its expression. We can't change our genetic makeup, but there are many steps we can take that will help us make the most of what we've been given. Visit the library, read books, shuffle through museums, watch documentaries, take a class, ask questions. The list is endless.

Learning isn't limited to the classroom. If you're serious about making the most of your mental potential, you can make a difference. Join a discussion group or begin one on a topic of interest to you, become a puzzle enthusiast, learn a new skill, learn a new word from the dictionary every day, misplace your calculator. Don't waste your potential; develop it and use it to change your world.

Wise men store up knowledge.

PROVERBS 10:14

147

IF I REALLY WANTED TO
MAKE A DIFFERENCE,
I WOULD . . .

VOTE

No vote—no voice.

I n South Africa, the right to vote is considered to be a priceless privilege. So dear is it that voters would rather risk their lives than stay away from the polls. That used to be the case in America, but scandal, corruption, and a money-hungry political system have left many feeling that their votes can't really make a difference.

Voting is one of the dearest duties and privileges of a free, democratic society. If for no other reason, cast your vote as a point of principle and out of respect for those who have paid the ultimate price for our freedom. Political reform will never come if responsible men and women bow out of the process. Go to the polls and let your voice be heard.

Do your duty, and leave the rest to heaven.

PIERRE CORNEILLE

IF I REALLY WANTED TO
MAKE A DIFFERENCE,
I WOULD . . .

LEARN NOT TO PROCRASTINATE

PROCRASTINATION ROBS US OF OUR BEST.

Procrastination threatens our sanity, weakens our relationships, limits our accomplishments, wastes our potential, and robs us of our time. It stresses us out and leaves us exhausted. That's the *bad* news! The good news is that procrastination is really just a lack of self-discipline—and fortunately, self-discipline can be learned.

If you're prone to procrastinate, there are many steps you can take to get this ugly monkey off your back. You can begin by making a realistic schedule and working hard to stick with it. You will have some early failures, but don't give up. In time, you will find it less daunting to stay the course. Another good strategy is to give yourself a time limit for making a decision or dealing with a certain situation. Tomorrow never comes, so be specific. Procrastinate no longer! Start fighting for your freedom—today.

Procrastination is the thief of time.

EDWARD YOUNG

IF I REALLY WANTED TO
MAKE A DIFFERENCE,
I WOULD . . .

SHOW
LOVE

LOVE IS A VERB.

How do you respond when your spouse bounces a check? Or your teenager backs the car through the garage door? How about when your neighbor's dog eats your petunias? Responding in love doesn't mean failing to hold others accountable for their actions, but it does mean forgiving quickly and refusing to hold a grudge.

The Bible says that "real" love has these qualities: It is patient and kind, never boastful, proud, or envious. It isn't rude or self-seeking. It doesn't get mad easily or keep a record of wrongs. It is never happy to see evil triumph and always rejoices when the truth is told. It protects, trusts, hopes, and perseveres. So pure is love that the Bible says it never fails. Determine to walk in love each day. You are sure to make a great difference in the lives of all those you encounter.

If I speak in the tongues of men and of angels, but have not love, I am only a resounding gong or a clanging symbol.

1 CORINTHIANS 13:1

IF I REALLY WANTED TO
MAKE A DIFFERENCE,
I WOULD . . .

CAREFULLY
CONSIDER
THE ADVICE
I'M GIVEN

LISTEN TO ADVICE WILLINGLY; ACT ON IT CAUTIOUSLY.

Advice is not in short supply. Everywhere we turn someone is trying to tell us where to shop, what type of car to buy, where to invest our money, whom to vote for, how to raise our children, and much more. The question is, how do we know what advice to take? If the advice happens to be good, it can save us time, money, maybe even our lives. But if it happens to be bad, we can find ourselves in a world of hurt.

The most important thing to remember about advice is to sleep on it. Give yourself time to process and evaluate it. Ask yourself the following questions: Does the advice giver have a track record of giving good advice? Does he or she have all the information needed to properly evaluate the situation? Is it possible that the advice giver has a vested interest or hidden agenda? Everyone makes the mistake of acting on bad advice from time to time. But you can make a real difference by considering all advice carefully.

Advice is a stranger; if welcome he stays for the night; if not welcome he returns home the same day.

MALAGASY PROVERB

KEEP AN OPEN MIND

KEEP YOUR MIND OPEN TO LIFE'S GRAND POSSIBILITIES.

As a knee-jerk reaction to an "accept everything" trend of thought, many conservative thinkers have resolved to cling even tighter to their methodology. This is disturbing because the only way we can grow and influence our world is by opening our minds to new thoughts and possibilities.

Give your mind permission to grow and expand and think outside the box. It will keep you fresh and open to innovative ways of facilitating positive change. Of course, having an open mind does not mean opening your mind to every perverse imagination that comes knocking. But locking your mind up tight can put a cap on your creativity and bury the unique insights only you can provide. A closed mind is like a closed umbrella; it doesn't do anyone any good.

Where there is an open mind, there will always be a frontier.

CHARLES F. KETTERING

IF I REALLY WANTED TO
MAKE A DIFFERENCE,
I WOULD . . .

NEVER
BE A
LITTERBUG

LITTERING SPEAKS LOUDER THAN WORDS.

L itter itself is enough to raise the ire of those who respect the environment, but the message behind littering is even more disturbing. It says, "I don't give a rip about this place or anyone who lives here."

If you're in the habit of carelessly tossing your trash out the window or dumping your junk at the end of a rural road—if you have been living by the adage "Out of sight; out of mind"—your actions may be saying things your mind never intended. Mend your ways. Failing to respect God's creation and disregarding the well-being of others will ultimately cause you to lose respect for yourself. It's never too late to turn over a new leaf if you really want to make a difference.

Of one ill, come many.

PROVERB

IF I REALLY WANTED TO
MAKE A DIFFERENCE,
I WOULD . . .

THINK
RESPONSIBLY

ONLY YOU CAN CHANGE YOUR MIND.

The choices we make have a profound effect not only on our lives but also on the lives of those who know and love us. That is all the more reason to carefully consider the decisions we make and the consequences those decisions create. And yet, thinking responsibly is not as easy as it sounds, especially in a world filled with ambiguities. Responsible thinking requires a commitment to change, to align ourselves with established values.

Have your efforts to make a significant difference in the world been hindered by the consequences of poor judgment and careless actions? You can choose to practice responsible thinking. You will still make mistakes from time to time, but in the course of your life, your commitment will pay off. You will discover more and more opportunities to positively effect the world around you.

The strongest principle of growth lies in human choice.

GEORGE ELIOT

IF I REALLY WANTED TO
MAKE A DIFFERENCE,
I WOULD . . .

PUT MY LIFE INTO GOD'S HANDS

GOD'S PLANS ALWAYS SUCCEED!

God has a plan for each of our lives, a plan more exciting than anything we could think or imagine. Fulfilling that plan, however, requires a conscious choice to seek His direction and follow carefully the path He sets before us. It means spending time in quiet reverence before Him until we are able to hear and distinguish His voice.

The best possible way to make a difference in your life and the lives of those you love is to actively pursue the plan God has created especially for you. The best way to leave a lasting legacy for those who will come after you is to commit your life to God and work together with Him to fulfill that plan. It is the only perfect formula for success. Open your heart and receive all He has for you.

"With God all things are possible."

MATTHEW 19:26

ALSO AVAILABLE IN THIS SERIES:

If I Really Wanted to Simplify my Life, I Would . . .
If I Really Wanted to Be Happy, I Would . . .
If I Really Wanted to Lose Weight, I Would . . .
If I Really Wanted to Have a Great Marriage, I Would . . .
If I Really Wanted to Be a Great Friend, I Would . . .
If I Really Wanted to Grow Closer to God, I Would . . .
If I Really Wanted to Beat Stress, I Would . . .

If you have enjoyed this book, or if it has impacted your life, we would love to hear from you.

Please contact us at:

info@honorbooks.com